It's Not Even Past

by

William G. Hill

Copyright © William G. Hill

All rights reserved. No part of this publication may be reproduced, distributed, or transmitted in any form or by any means, including photocopying, recording, or other electronic or mechanical methods, without the prior written permission of the publisher, except in the case of brief quotations embodied in critical reviews and certain other noncommercial uses permitted by copyright law.

ISBN-978-1-951300-33-3

Liberation's Publishing LLC
West Point - Mississippi

Dedication

For

Anna

Mama

Charles Ingram

Sally Askew

Members of the Poetry Society of Tennessee

Members of the Mississippi Poetry Society

Members of Byhalia Christian Writers

Acknowledgments

I want to thank the following folks:

The members of The Thursday Afternoon Mid-Town Writing Circle who read and added so much to all this work.

Most of all Anna Hill, my wife, editor, encourager, and the real talent in our family.

Table of Contents

Tuff Nut 7
Because Someone Told Me 8
It Happens Every Year 10
Tales From the Palmer Woods 11
The Fine Dining Capital of Mississippi 12
Woody's Place 13
In the Town Where I Grew Up 14
Rosemary 15
The Last Rebel 16
Mt. Zion About 1955 17
Eulogy With a Chuck Berry Duck Walk 18
Rustic Nocturne: 20
Ruth Ann 21
When We Came Alive in 1965 22
Gerald 23
Three Tigers 24
   Some Poems That Were Honored 25
Pandemic Limerick 28
The Preacher III 29
2020 30
Discourse on the Relative Merits of Employment 31
Justice? 32
A New Standard 33
One Who Never Stood in Water 34
Notes 35

Tuff Nut

Mama and Daddy took me onetime
    down to Mr. Finger's store.
I guess I had, but don't remember
    ever going there before.
It was nearing time to start back
    to school and we had meager means.
But every year Mama saw to it
    that I got some new blue jeans.
Getting bran new clothes every new
    school year was a big part of life,
because if you bought two pairs of
    Tuff Nutt jeans you got a free pocketknife.
Now, I carry a Buck and know
    those free knives were not that great,
but I never would have believed
    that when I was seven or eight.
All I knew was that I had a
    pocketknife of my very own,
like Daddy and Papa Hill and
    my cousins who were grown.
There are so many rites of passage
    in every little boy's life.
One of those for me was getting
    my first Tuff Nutt pocketknife.

Because Someone Told Me

So many there are that do not know.
So many there are that do not seem to care.
How can they claim the claims of the faith they claim
and yet not know who they are or where they came from.

There was a cross, so long ago and far away,
and a man falsely accused. I know about Him
because someone told me.

There was a flag that once flew through a dark night
And a man held prisoner. I know about him
because someone told me.

I know where Jefferson, Mississippi is,
I know where the Land of Oz is,
because someone told me.

I know that "Everything is up to date in Kansas City."
I know that "there's trouble in River City"
because someone told me.

I know how to tie shoes,
I know how to make cornbread,
because someone told me.

Mama and Papa, Maw and Paw, and others,
some I saw a little, some were gone before I got here.
I know them all
because someone told me.

So many there are that do not know.
So many there are that do not seem to care.
I must not sit in judgement of them.
They have not been told as I have been.
They were never told who they are or where they came from.

It Happens Every Year

The light pastels of spring are past.
The greens of summer did not last.
Fall's red and gold have gone away,
now is the time of winter's gray.

With days so short and nights so long,
I wish to hear the robin's song,
but spring will come again I know.
I see butter cups in the snow.

Tales From the Palmer Woods

Around Ripley in the spring of the year,
it would not be long until you would hear
scary stories that would always feature
a monster called The Palmer Woods Creature.

Some said it was big and black like a cat,
Others said it was brown, hairy, and fat.
It had big eyes that would shine in the night,
long sharp claws and teeth just made for a fight.

My sister saw it while on a date.
Mama asked, "You were in the woods that late?"
Well, Sis changed the subject right there and then
and never brought up The Creature again!

There was a fellow down near Cotton Plant,
said he saw it chasing his old maid aunt.
I know it is true, there is evidence,
that thing knocked over an eight-foot board fence!

Don't stop for nothing if you're there about,
folks went in those woods and never came out.
Now, I never saw it with my own eye,
but I know the boys at Jackson's Pool Hall don't lie.

The Fine Dining Capital of Mississippi

There is something I would still like to do,
run out to Coleman's for some Bar-B-Q,
or The Cream Cup for a hamburger steak
and top it off with a chocolate milk shake.
The great cheeseburgers at Fox's Truck Stop,
and those Drug Store hot dogs were hard to top.
Lois and Hattie served big plate lunches.
Mr. Lawrence fried burgers in bunches!
The Barn's burgers were made mostly of dough,
so, for real home cooking see Ruth Renfroe.
Nanny ran a place next to the Co-op
where the folks at Blue Bell would always stop.
Conn's, Bell's Drive-in, Big Star and Mug 'n' Cone
always had a crowd, you were not alone.
Fifty years ago, when you went to eat
Ripley was a place that was hard to beat.
I will name one more café, if you please,
don't forget Alexander's Frosty Freeze.

Woody's Place

We used to have some great jam sessions
    in the back of Woody's music store.
I often wonder, is there a place
    where folks jam like that anymore?
I hung out there because, though I had
    little talent, I loved playing the drums.
We called ourselves professional
    musicians but mama called us bums!
Some of the guys were pretty good
    players but many others were like me.
Those who would spend hours in practice
    just to achieve mediocrity.
Someone would go to the piano,
    sit down and begin playing a song,
then everybody in there would
    grab an instrument and play along.
Some of the bunch liked country music,
    and others were into rock and roll,
every once in a while, a guy
    would sit in who would add a little soul.
We did not even know what to
    call the kind of music we were playing,
but whatever it was, we were proud
    of what we thought we were saying.
Some of the boys still get together,
    most of us have gone our separate ways,
but in my mind, nothing will top
    the sound we made back in the good old days.

In the Town Where I Grew Up

In the town where I grew up,
on the south side of The Square,
was a drug store and soda fountain,
and us kids hung out there.

On the east side was a pool hall
where we went on Saturday night,
but J.M. would not let us stay
if we were going to fight.

Finger's store was on the north side.
I'll remember all my life,
if you bought a pare of Tuff-Nutt jeans there,
you got a free pocketknife.

On the west side was
 King's Firestone and Ma Tate,
 also, Renfroe's café,
where a lot of times we ate.

I drove around The Square last month,
as I did my heart raced.
All those places that I loved
had been replaced.

Rosemary

Was it Nettleton, Shannon, Kossuth,
Boonville, Baldwin, or Calhoun City?
I can't remember where we were going,
getting old is such a pity.

It was a regular Friday night
and we were on the road.
My friend and I, his mom and dad,
his sister and her guest made up the load.

We stopped by her house to pick her up,
my friend's sister's friend that is,
when I first saw her, I couldn't help but think,
how could anyone be as pretty as this.

I got to know her a little better
through our high school and college days.
Though we never were what's called close friends
she grew more beautiful in many ways.

There are many in our lives
who make it a little more fun.
I think I speak for all when
I say, Rosemary was one.

The Last Rebel

You can't get to Falkner
on the railroad Falkner built.
They dug it up after
the GM&O turned into the IC,
and the IC turned into the CN.

I was standing in Papa Hill's yard
with him and Daddy and my uncles.
We heard a train whistle.
My uncle said, "That's the last one."
I asked, "Last what?"
"The last Rebel", Papa said.
"There won't be anymore."

The next night I heard a train.
"Daddy, I thought y'all said
they wouldn't be no more?"
"That's just an old freight train."

I didn't know until much later
how much the world,
our world,
had changed in one day's time.

Mt. Zion About 1955

Have you ever been to a country church
revival meeting? They had them two times
a day back then, and they lasted about
a week. The ones in the afternoons were
in the hottest part of the day. The ones
at night were not much cooler. Sometimes it
would come up a cloud right before the night
service started. Every time it did the
preacher-- they always got somebody to
be our preacher while they were having the
revival that wasn't our regular
preacher-- would say, "Sing 'Showers of Blessings,'"
and grin real big like nobody had said
that at every revival meeting, when
it rained, for the last hundred years. Now days
they say those old-time preachers preached hell
so
hot you could feel the heat, but I don't think
it was that. It was really that hot!
We had no air conditioners back then!

Eulogy With a Chuck Berry Duck Walk

We know what we have done.
We know Adam's curse.
We know the wages we have earned.
We accept the end of our "mad man's tale".

Yet we say, "Why?",
not with a fist shaking in the face of God.
Yet we say, "Why?",
because we would understand.

We have faith, we have trust,
but we ask, "Why?"
Was his music too good for us?
Did the angels need an ax man?

We hear the same voice of the Poet,
the one who pronounced the curse, say,
"There is a time to weep…
and a time to sing."

We sing and play knowing
what it would be without love.
We sing and play knowing
there will be no sounding brass or clashing cymbals in this place.

We have not come to weep.
We have come to sing.
We have not come to wring our hands.

We have come to clap our hands.

We have not come to ask,
"Do the good die young?"
We have come to say,
"Any good man's life is too short."

We say together in faith,
"Praise Him from whom all blessings flow."
We say together in joy,
"Hail! Hail! Rock and roll!"

Rustic Nocturne:

Heard through an open window in summertime

Dogs barking and howling.
At what? Something real? Something imagined?
Mostly other dogs.
Lonesome blues accompanied by a bottle neck guitar
as the protector of each house or farm
stands to give a warning, or
to join in the jam session.

The rumble and the roar of The Rebel is
muted by distance until it becomes only a gentle hum.
A hum so soft it goes unnoticed, until
the whistle plays its blue yodel
as the train nears the crossing.

When all else is quiet,
whip-poor-wills, owls, and bob white
begin their call and response.
A southern gospel counterpoints
to the minor key blues of howls and whistles.

Just before day,
trucks on the highway start practicing their scales.
Moving up and up
each gear a higher octave,
until they reach the weigh station at Walnut.

Ruth Ann

I am looking at a sixty
year old picture of me and you.
I still remember that time our
folks took us to the Memphis Zoo.
Now we are old, you are gray and
I do not have much hair at all,
but I thank the Lord I still have
my first friend from when I was small.
We'll each have another birthday
this November and December.
but few can say they have been friends
as long as they can remember.

When We Came Alive in 1965

The singers pranced upon the stage.
There were only four.
The house was built to bounce
a ball across a wooden floor.
Two live on and two are gone
to that Cavern in the sky.
So, tear it down, this house so round.
it's dead no use to cry.
Can things be made to rise again
that once were alive?
Can hearts ever return again
to 1965?

Gerald

My cousin.
My first playmate.
My mentor.
My granter of all the knowledge
    of all the things boys should know.
My tormentor at times.
My protector at times.
My role model.
My source of jokes that Mama and Aunt Juanita
    would have whipped us for if they heard us telling them.
My first hero.
My hero still.

Three Tigers

Green leaves on trees
against a clear blue sky--
green leaves on cotton stalks
with bolls not yet open--
the late summer sun
beating down bright and hot—
and the Tiger limped away.

Brown, red, and yellow leaves—
white, heaps of cotton, clouds—
brown leafless cotton stalks
with white bolls ready for the pickers—
the autumn afternoon sun giving
way to the harvest moon—
and the Tiger crawled away.

Bare black tree branches
against a gray November sky—
gray and brown cut-over cotton fields—
and they carried the Tiger away!

Some Poems That Were Honored

The previous poems came from my heart and my recollections of growing up in in Tippah County. They do not even come close to presenting all the people, places, events, and sometimes romanticized memories of growing up.

What follows are a few poems that I have been honored and blessed to have others notice. I hope you appreciate them as well.

Pandemic Limerick

There was a girl named Maxine.
She would not take a vaccine.
She said, "Listen folks,
the pandemic's a hoax."
Now she sleeps in the church yard serene.

The Preacher III

How, with the world falling apart,
can my heart say, "Of The I sing…"?
I can because the wise men say
there is a time for everything.

A time to sing, a time to laugh
and a time set aside for crying.
A time to love a time to live
and even a time for dying.

The judge is in the courthouse but
justice and truth are not his goal.
The preacher in the church gains the
world but only to lose his soul.

Each of us will die like a dog.
We will again return to dust,
but I can say," of the I sing….",
 You are the only one to trust.

I must rejoice in what I do,
in the work you have had me bring.
No one but you can see the end
because of that "Of the I sing…."!

2020

For freedom and justice many are yearning.
Schools are closed no one is learning.

No truth in the temple, no justice at court.
The ones who lead us are not discerning.

Alaska is melting, Louisiana has floods.
No snow in Vermont and California is burning.

Soldiers march, sailors sail, airman fly.
Our young die because turmoil is churning.

Another trip around the sun we have almost made.
The earth on its axis has kept turning.

Discourse on the Relative Merits of Employment

Find a vocation you love, so
you will not be a working slob.
If you find work you love to do,
it is a hobby, not a job.

Find some work that satisfies, so
you can put your heart into it.
If people really liked to work,
they would need no pay to do it.

Find some noble endeavor, so
you will have a place in the sun.
If you ain't too tired on payday
grab the money and have some fun.

Justice?

What do dark skinned people need to overcome their plight?
That is easy, all they need is just to be white.

What do women need these days to be all they can?
That is easy, all they need is to be a man.

When folks are held back because of their faith what can they do?
That is easy, as long as they are not a Jew.

Pull up by your bootstraps. No more singing the blues.
That is easy, all you need is just a pair of shoes.

A New Standard

Why do we wave a rebel flag?
Is it to brag
on past glory?
That's the story.
Past glory that is, we contend,
gone with the wind,
and all we say
is look away.
Raise a flag that does not divide.
Let go of pride.
Let it be said,
we look ahead.

One Who Never Stood in Water

There are those who pass through our lives
without ever leaving a trace.
As if they stood in a river,
they're gone and nothing marks the place.
For as quickly as they start to
move, the water begins to flow.
Nothing, not even footprints,
is left behind them when they go.

But others come and then move on
and where they stood, an empty space.
In our hearts we know there'll never
be found one, who can fill their place.
The ones who by the grace of God
turn their hearts and minds to doing good.
The ones we long to see again,
for in water they never stood.

Notes

Tuff Nutt:
a merging of many years, we all did it.

Because Someone Told Me:
Was first written as a thank you note to Mama, also known as Jewel, Aunt Jewel, Ms. Jewel, mom, and mother, for all she taught me.

Tales from The Palmer Woods:
Just one of many tall tales we heard growing up.

The Fine Dining Capital of Mississippi
Woody's Place
In the Town Where I Grow Up:
Are about places I remember most of them are gone.

Rosemary:
Rosemary Butler left us at a time when a good number of our friends from the 60's left us. I chose her because she was the one of them that I could remember the exact time I first saw her.

The Last Rebel:
This is what happened, as I remember it, the night the last Rebel came through Falkner.
I have been honored by the folks at the Falkner Mississippi Heritage Museum who have asked that this become their official poem. I share ownership of this intellectual property with them.

I am the "self-proclaimed" poet laureate of Falkner.

Mt. Zion About 1955:
I could not present memories without some of this place.

Eulogy With a Chuck Berry Duck Walk:
This was written to honor my friend Buddy Grisham. He went home in 2020, a victim of Covid 19. A bunch of his musician friends got together for a tribute at The Ripley Sports Grill. Many remembered my drum playing and asked me to write something.

Rustic Nocturne:
We've all heard it.

Ruth Ann:
I can't remember when Ruth Ann Jones Griffin was not my friend.

When We Came Alive in 1965:
This is a recollection of the time Nell, Walter, Jan Holliday Tidwell, Becky Holliday Waldon and I went to Memphis to see the Beatles. Eddie Morton had a ticket but Billy Sewan, put a stop to that. A story for another time. It took place in 1966 but that does not rhyme with alive.

Gerald:
Yes, Gerald Hill is still my hero forever! This however is a tribute to all my wonderful cousins.

Three Tigers:
Is about driving to Ole Miss for football games. The Rebels beat Memphis, Auburn and LSU that Year. Hotty Toddy!!!

SOME POEMS THAT WERE HONORED:
I have been blessed over the years to have had many who helped me along. These poems which have been judged by my fellow poets as having some merit, I dedicate to those people.

The Cover:
I created the art for the cover from a photograph taken by Jack Elliot. It shows us where the "…railroad that Falkner built…" stops now just north of Ripley.

The Title:
From this quote, "The past is not dead, it's not even past". —William Faulkner